The Healthy Chocoholic

THE HEALTHY CHOCOHOLIC

dawn parker

The Healthy Chocoholic

Copyright © 2015 by Dawn Parker

To contact the publisher, visit
www.dawnjparker.com

To contact the author, visit
www.dawnjparker.com

Paperback ISBN: 978-0-9967857-0-9

Electronic ISBN: 978-0-9967857-1-6

Printed in the United States of America

Cover photo: Christy Maiquez
Cover design: Ashley Ruggirello
Book design: Ashley Ruggirello

Table of Contents

INTRODUCTION
Who this book is for

This book is for people who want to be healthy and eat healthy, but don't want to deprive themselves of the pleasure that good food has to offer. Like many of you, I love to eat. And I believe that food is medicine. Combining my love of eating and my knowledge of how healthy food nourishes the body led me to create delicious recipes that are also nutritious.

As a health coach, I have seen many people who are intolerant of certain foods. My youngest son has Celiac disease so he cannot have gluten. I avoid gluten and soy due to my Hashimoto's thyroiditis. I have worked with many clients to help them uncover food intolerances that had caused years of symptoms. These intolerances often involved hard to avoid foods like dairy, gluten, nuts and soy.

One client of mine, who suffered from Crohn's disease for over 20 years, experienced life-changing relief from her symptoms after removing gluten from her diet. Another client, who was extremely hesitant about trying an elimination diet, discovered that gluten and dairy had caused her years of bloating and stomach pain. Another discovered that lowering her sugar intake nearly eliminated her fatigue and daily need for afternoon naps.

Things like gluten, dairy and processed sugar are extremely prevalent in our food supply, so removing them can be a challenge for many people. This led me to spend a lot of time creating delicious recipes for my clients that were free of gluten, dairy, soy, peanuts, corn, eggs, grains and other things that weren't working for them. These recipes made living without the foods that were causing them issues so much easier.

As a mom, and working with clients who have children of their own, creating recipes that would pass the kid test has been key. Although these recipes are healthier than most chocolate treats, all have been taste-tested by the most honest of all critics— children.

Several clients told me that my recipes needed to be shared with the world. They couldn't believe how I made healthy food taste SO good. They were pleasantly surprised that their children were eating healthy foods they had never eaten before. They made my recipes to bring to parties, and no one could tell they were healthy. They said I should write a cookbook. So I did.

I decided to start with my favorite food of all—chocolate. I have had a love affair with chocolate my entire life. Even as a child, I preferred dark chocolate over milk chocolate. Years later, when I discovered that dark chocolate was much healthier, I made eating it a daily ritual. Whether it is a few squares of my favorite store-bought variety or enjoying the results of my latest cookbook creation, rarely does a day go by that I don't indulge in healthy chocolate.

All the recipes start with the healthiest ingredients, which you'll learn more about in this book. Additionally, the recipes are free of refined white sugar and are sweetened with more natural ingredients, such as maple syrup, honey, dates and coconut sugar. These healthy ingredients come together to bring you decadent chocolate treats you can feel good about eating and making for your family. Whether or not you have a food intolerance, if you want a healthier approach to chocolate, this cookbook is for you.

About Dawn

Dawn Parker is a Certified Health Coach who supports women, couples and families in learning how to use nutrition to improve their health. She received her training at the Institute for Integrative Nutrition (IIN). Using her specialized knowledge, she helps clients feel great by uncovering hidden food intolerances and helping them transition into a healthy eating lifestyle. Dawn's commitment to creating customized recipes for healthy and DELICIOUS food has helped her transform the health of many clients.

Dawn lives in Zionsville, Indiana with her husband and two young sons. She works with clients all throughout the United States, both one on one and in online groups.

Learn more about Dawn's health coaching programs at www.dawnjparker.com. And follow her for health and wellness tips at www.facebook.com/ dawnjparkerhealthcoach.

TESTIMONIALS

I always thought I was a relatively healthy eater until I started working with Dawn. She taught me a lot about our food supply and how to make better choices for me and my family. **Dawn helped me achieve a number of goals by providing realistic solutions that worked with my busy lifestyle as a full-time working mother of two small children.** My job requires quite a bit of travel, and Dawn provided solutions for healthy eating on the road as well. I had always read food labels in the past, but Dawn helped me understand what the ingredients were and the impact they could have on my body, which ultimately helped me cut out processed foods. This wasn't as hard as I thought, because Dawn provided healthy alternatives to some of my favorite not-so-healthy foods.

Dawn's recipes helped me get my extremely picky toddler to enjoy nutritious foods that were easy to make. Neither my daughter or I liked beans or nuts. With Dawn's recipes—like walnut brownies and garbanzo bean cookies—we've learned to like them! I once brought her chocolate-covered rice cereal bars to a party, and everyone loved them and could not believe how healthy they were! I have also incorporated healthy smoothies into my family's diet on a regular basis, which is an easy way to sneak nutrients into meals without hearing any complaints!

The recipes that Dawn shared with me were simple and easy to follow, which was key for someone who doesn't have a lot of free time. While she still provided me with healthy suggestions for prepackaged foods, I now try to make as much as I can at home. **I continue to make several of the recipes I received, including granola bars, cookies and homemade chocolate. Working with Dawn helped me make long-lasting lifestyle changes.** Not only did we focus on healthy eating, but she also helped me reduce overall toxins in my household. **I am looking forward to trying Dawn's new recipes in this much anticipated cookbook!**

Sheila Newth | Newton, MA

Before working with Dawn I suffered from years of stomach pain without knowing the cause. Even after multiple attempts at uncovering the root of the problem, it wasn't until I worked with Dawn that I realized I had food intolerances. She helped me identify foods like dairy and gluten that were causing me these digestive issues. Once I removed these foods, I no longer had bloating and pain after every meal. I realized how much this impacted me when I went out to eat with a friend. I ordered a big antipasto salad (free of dairy and gluten) and my friend ordered eggplant parmesan. After we finished dinner, I was full of energy and ready to go shopping. Unfortunately, my friend felt so terrible and tired that she needed to go home and lie down. I have come to appreciate how the right and wrong foods can dramatically impact how it makes people feel.

To make eliminating dairy and gluten easier, Dawn shared many of her healthy recipes which my whole family, including three young boys, love. Some of our favorite recipes are her brownies and her no-bake bites.

One of my personal goals while working with Dawn was to lose a little weight. With her fitness suggestions, stress reduction strategies, and nutrition advice, I lost 12 pounds and 8 inches.

If you are looking to make some changes in your life and don't know where to start, Dawn is an amazing coach and can help you succeed.

Janine Gordon | Plymouth, MA

I've had thyroid issues for over 20 years. In all that time, even though I saw many primary care doctors and even endocrinologists, no one ever tested me for Hashimoto's thyroiditis. When I stared working with Dawn, she suggested I get my antibodies tested to find out if I had this autoimmune condition. When the test came back positive, I couldn't believe that none of my doctors had ever suggested it.

Then I learned that there are certain foods that don't work for me, like gluten and soy. I thought removing them from my diet was going to be horrible. No bread? No waffles? No muffins? I'm happy to say Dawn has shown me many ways to switch to better options of my favorite foods, rather than exclude them forever. I've learned that it's not about going without, it's about making a few changes and choosing healthier foods that work better for my body. Dawn has shared some wonderful recipes with me. I love her healthy waffles and her trick for a lower sugar maple syrup. We also love her cookies, healthy pie crust and lots of other recipes.

My husband is very supportive and does most of the cooking, and he was able to make all of the recipes Dawn provided. She even took us on a health food store tour where we learned to read labels to find healthy foods without gluten and soy. My kids have benefited from these changes too. We've removed a lot of processed foods and the kids can't even tell the difference! They enjoy the healthy foods and recipes we are now eating.

I've had some great improvements in my health as a result of working with Dawn. I've lost ten pounds, and continue to lose as I stick with this way of eating. I often experienced fatigue before, but now it's easier to get out of bed in the morning and I have more energy throughout the day. My inflammatory labs have greatly improved and the joint pain that plagued me for years is almost gone. My blood sugar numbers, like average glucose and A1c, have improved and so have my thyroid labs. I was having frequent migraines despite being on a daily prevention medicine. Now I have been getting them so infrequently that I was able to come off the medication and am doing well without it. I was also able to stop taking hormones due to an improvement in symptoms and in my labs.

I'm so thankful for all that I've learned from Dawn, and it makes me want to learn even more.

Melissa Ingersoll | Brownsburg, IN

My name is Allyson Sloan. I was diagnosed with Crohn's disease at the age of 13. I have taken every available Crohn's immunosuppressant as well as two study drugs. I have had surgery to remove part of my small intestine. I was hospitalized in September of 2014 with an intestinal obstruction. At that point in my life, I felt like I would never be well again. Aside from more surgery, the gastroenterologists really had nothing new to offer me.

I met Dawn Parker in 2012. I knew she was a health coach, but didn't really think she could help someone with my disease. I am a registered nurse and my husband is a physician. Up to this point, we had followed the advice of medical professionals. After the bowel obstruction in 2014, I was very depressed. I knew I didn't want any more surgery, **so I decided to meet with Dawn. It was the best decision I have ever made for my health. With Dawn's guidance, I have completely changed my diet and my life. I didn't think feeling normal, energetic and healthy were even options for me. Dawn proved me wrong.** In the past year of seeing Dawn, I have been able to get off and remain off steroids and have had far fewer bouts of abdominal pain. Furthermore, my inflammatory labs are continually improving. For example, my calprotectin improved from 900 down to 88. She has shown me how to change my diet to support intestinal health.

My husband and I considered ourselves to be "foodies." We loved trying new restaurants. Sadly, every time I ate out I would suffer the consequences. Now we cook at home using many of Dawn's recipes. My kids love the chocolate chip cookies, hot chocolate and granola. My husband enjoys the Thai coconut rice and pumpkin soup. **Dawn has helped me create restaurant quality meals using only healthy ingredients.** As a result, we found the transition to gluten-free eating to be much easier than expected. We never feel like we are compromising.

With Dawn's help, I feel great for the first time in 27 years. I have energy to enjoy my husband, children and career. Our entire family has benefited from Dawn Parker's expertise.

Allyson Sloan | Zionsville, IN

THE HEALTH BENEFITS OF CHOCOLATE

Dark chocolate is one of my favorite healthy indulgences. Not only is it delicious, but if you buy the right kind, it can be healthy for you. There are several health benefits to cacao, but, unfortunately, not all chocolate is created equal when it comes to this important ingredient. Chocolate is made from cacao beans, which are the seed of a fruit that comes from a jungle tree in tropical countries near the equator. After being removed from their pods, cacao beans are typically fermented, dried and then roasted. After the

skins are removed, what remains is the cacao nib. These nibs can be ground into a paste for making chocolate, or separated into the fat, known as cacao butter, and the solids, which are milled into cacao powder. You will see both cacao nibs and cacao powder in many of the recipes in this cookbook.

Cacao offers a lot of nutritional benefits. It is high in magnesium, and magnesium deficiency is becoming increasingly common. Magnesium is responsible for hundreds of enzymatic reactions in the body. Some of the benefits of magnesium are heart health, bone health, muscle relaxation and healthy bowel function. Cacao is an excellent source of iron, vitamin C and fiber. It is also a good source of PEA (also known as the love hormone), zinc, manganese, tryptophan, serotonin and theobromine. Cacao has appetite suppressing qualities and is considered to be a superfood.

Cacao is higher in antioxidants than most foods in the world, including blueberries, pomegranate, acai berries and red wine. Antioxidants protect us from age-related health conditions and illnesses.

Most people are more familiar with cocoa than cacao, so what is the difference? Cocoa is usually cacao powder treated with alkali to remove bitterness, which is called "dutching." This process removes many of the antioxidant flavanols and reduces the health benefits. To get the most health benefits out of a chocolate product, read the label and pass on those that have alkali or use dutch processing.

There are several other factors to consider when buying cacao powder, or when choosing a chocolate bar or chocolate chips. Unfortunately, cacao is a high pesticide crop.

To avoid consuming all of those pesticides, I recommend choosing organic. Also, the practice of forced child labor continues in some areas of the cacao trade, so look for the fair trade label.

If you can't find organic, watch for and avoid these ingredients, which are not labeled organic or non-GMO:

1. Sugar
Look for cane sugar or evaporated cane juice. When listed as "sugar," it is usually from GMO sugar beets.

2. Dairy
Milk, lactose, milk fat or other dairy ingredients, unless labeled otherwise, probably comes from cows fed GMOs.

3. Soy Lecithin
Unless otherwise labeled is also probably GMO.

4. Vanillin
This is not the same ingredient as vanilla, but usually a synthetic product.

5. Artificial Flavors

To get the most health benefits from cacao, choose chocolate bars and chips with a high cacao content—70% or more. This will not only result in getting a lot of the healthy cacao, but will also mean there is a lower sugar content, which makes it healthier as well. Check the amount of sugar grams per serving to be sure.

Sorry to be the bearer of bad news, but milk chocolate does not have the same health benefits as dark chocolate. Dairy can interfere with the body's ability to absorb healthy antioxidants in the cacao. Also, the addition of the dairy lowers the cacao content and raises the sugar content.

When selecting chocolate chips to use for the recipes in this book, select high quality chocolate to maintain the health impact of these recipes. Review the ingredient list and compare to make the healthiest choice. High quality chocolate should only have a small amount of ingredients and you should recognize them all. You'll pay a little more for the higher quality bars, chunks or chips, but the health benefits are worth the additional cost. And you can feel

better knowing that the treats you make will be providing nutrients for you and your family.

About The Recipes

All of the recipes in this book contain healthy ingredients and are lower in sugar than typical sweet treat recipes. Food intolerances are varied, so this list will help you determine if this book will fit your needs.

ALL of the recipes are free of:

Gluten
Dairy
Soy
Corn
Legumes, including peanuts
Refined white sugar

MOST of the recipes are:

Vegan
eggs are used in a few recipes, but the rest are vegan
Paleo
all recipes are gluten-free, but brown rice cereal and gluten-free oats are used in a few recipes

If you have allergies to certain tree nuts, many of the recipes can easily be adapted by swapping out for a different nut.

SHOPPING LIST

Below is a list of ingredients that are commonly used in the recipes in this book.

CACAO/CHOCOLATE

- Cacao nibs - raw, organic
- Cacao powder - raw, organic
- Chocolate chips - high cacao content; dairy, soy and gluten-free are preferred
- Dark chocolate bars - high cacao content; dairy, soy and gluten-free are preferred

COCONUT

- Unsweetened, shredded coconut
- Coconut flour
- Coconut milk - canned (BPA free), organic (not light)
- Coconut oil - unrefined, cold or expeller pressed and organic

NUTS AND SEEDS:

- Almond butter - 100%, no additional ingredients (crunchy and creamy)
- Almond milk - unsweetened
- Macadamia nuts
- Pecans
- Flaxseeds
- Walnuts

SWEETENERS:

- Coconut nectar
- Coconut sugar
- Medjool dates
- Honey - raw, local and/or organic if possible
- Maple syrup - 100% pure, grade B if possible

OTHER:

- Cinnamon, ceylon preferred
- Himalayan salt
- Vanilla (ground vanilla beans or pure vanilla extract)
- Brown rice cereal—the only ingredients should be brown rice and possibly a small amount of sweetener and salt
- Eggs - pastured and organic are best
- Gluten-free oats

Some recipes have other ingredients, but those that are frequently used are listed above.
These are the common ingredients used in my kitchen when making chocolate treats.

Cacao Nibs

Special note about cacao nibs:

Cacao nibs are added to a few of the smoothies in this book. The problem with using cacao nibs in smoothies is that they often sink to the bottom of the glass. To avoid this, try to use cacao nibs in thicker smoothie recipes. The thickness of the smoothie suspends the cacao nibs to evenly distribute them.

In addition, you can blend the nibs in bulk so they are smaller in size and don't tend to sink. To do this, pour the nibs into a small glass ball jar until it is about 3/4 full. Then pour them into a blender and pulse a few times until they are broken into smaller bits. They can be stored with the other non-refrigerated smoothie ingredients in the cupboard. See the picture to the left.

SMOOTHIES

Pictured: *Chocolate Pecan Pie Protein Smoothie*

Chocolate Coconut Cream Smoothie

This is a nice afternoon treat when you are looking for something sweet and filling enough to tide you over until dinner. Although it's less than 300 calories, the healthy fats, fiber and protein will fill you up without spiking your blood sugar, and will keep you satisfied for hours. It's also a great option when you're looking for a healthier or dairy-free version of chocolate milk.

Yield: 1 serving

3/4 cup almond milk
1/4 cup canned coconut cream*
1/2 date, pitted**
1 tbsp raw cacao powder
1 tbsp almond butter

*Coconut cream is the thick cream part of canned coconut milk. For this you want regular coconut milk, not light, in a can that is free of BPA. Open the can and on top you should have coconut cream, with the coconut milk below.

**Use the whole date if you have a sweet tooth or if it is a small date.

1. Add all the ingredients to a blender.
2. If your almond butter is unsalted, add a pinch of Himalayan salt.
3. Blend until the dates are smooth.

Chocolate Coconut Protein Smoothie

When having your smoothie as a breakfast or after your workout, protein is important. This creamy smoothie has lots of protein and healthy fats with no added sugar.

Yield: 1 serving

1/4 cup canned coconut cream*
1/4 cup coconut water, chilled
1/2 cup water
1 scoop vegan chocolate protein powder
Pinch of cacao nibs - optional

*Coconut cream is the thick cream part of canned coconut milk. For this you want regular coconut milk, not light, in a can that is free of BPA. Open the can and on top you should have coconut cream, with the coconut milk below.

1. For best results chill the coconut cream and the coconut water.
2. Add the first four ingredients to a blender and blend until smooth.
3. Pour into a glass.
4. Sprinkle cacao nibs over the top, if using.

Peppermint Patty Protein Smoothie

This protein smoothie makes a great breakfast, snack or post-workout meal. With a rich chocolate taste and creamy texture, it is sweetened with the natural fruit sugars from a date. Pure peppermint extract gives it a cool, minty flavor.

Yield: 1 serving

1 cup almond milk
1 scoop vegan chocolate protein
* powder*
*1 tbsp canned coconut cream**
1 tbsp freshly ground flax seed -
* optional*
2 tbsp raw cacao powder
1 Medjool date, pitted
1/4 tsp peppermint extract

*Coconut cream is the thick cream part of canned coconut milk. For this you want regular coconut milk, not light, in a can that is free of BPA. Open the can and on top you should have coconut cream, with the coconut milk below.

1. Add all the ingredients to a blender and blend until smooth.

Chocolate Chip Protein Smoothie

Frozen banana gives an ice-cream like texture and sweetness to this simple chocolate chip smoothie.

Yield: 1 serving

1 cup almond milk
1/2 frozen banana
1 scoop vegan chocolate protein
* powder*
1 tbsp cacao nibs + a few extra

1. Add the almond milk, banana and protein powder to a blender and process until smooth.

2. Add 1 tbsp of the cacao nibs and blend until the nibs are small bits.

3. Top with a few extra nibs, if desired.

Note: To freeze bananas, peel first, then cut into small pieces. Spread out on a cookie sheet and place in the freezer. Once frozen, transfer the banana slices to a freezer-safe glass container. The smaller pieces of frozen banana won't stick together and will be easier for the blender to process.

Chocolate Cranberry Protein Smoothie

Enjoy the wonderful health benefits of cranberries and cacao in this delicious protein smoothie.

Yield: 1 serving

1 cup of filtered water
1/2 frozen banana
1/2 cup fresh or frozen cranberries
1 scoop vegan chocolate
  protein powder
1 tbsp raw cacao powder

1. Add all the ingredients to a blender and blend until the bits of cranberry skin are small.

Notes: To freeze bananas, peel first, then cut into small pieces. Spread out on a cookie sheet and place in the freezer. Once frozen, transfer the banana slices to a freezer-safe glass container. The smaller pieces of frozen banana won't stick together and will be easier for the blender to process.

Cranberries are in season in the fall and are hard to get unprocessed at other times of the year. To enjoy cranberries in your smoothies all year long, stock up in the fall when they are plentiful and store in your freezer for several months.

Post-Workout Chocolate Cherry Smoothie

After a workout, cherries have been shown in some studies to reduce muscle soreness. Cherries are a key ingredient in this post-workout smoothie. In addition, coconut water contains key electrolytes that are lost in an intense workout. And finally, the protein powder provides protein for muscle repair.

Yield: 1 serving

1/3 cup coconut water
2/3 cup almond milk
1/3 cup frozen cherries
1 scoop vegan chocolate protein
*   powder*
Pinch of ground cacao nibs -
*   optional*

1. Add all the ingredients to a blender and blend until smooth.

2. For a little crunch, top with some ground cacao nibs.

Chocolate Almond Butter Smoothie

Always a popular combination, this smoothie matches chocolate with almond butter and is sweetened with the natural sugars of a date. For more of a frosty treat, swap the date out for 1/2 a frozen banana.

Yield: 1 serving

1 cup almond milk
1 Medjool date, pitted (OR 1/2
*   frozen banana)*
1 tbsp almond butter
1 tbsp raw cacao powder

1. Add all the ingredients to a blender.

2. If your almond butter is unsalted, add a pinch of Himalayan salt.

3. Blend until the date is smooth.

Note: To freeze bananas, peel first, then cut into small pieces. Spread out on a cookie sheet and place in the freezer. Once frozen, transfer the banana slices to a freezer-safe glass container. The smaller pieces of frozen banana won't stick together and will be easier for the blender to process.

Chocolate-Covered Strawberry Smoothie

Chocolate-covered strawberries are a classic treat enjoyed by many people. This smoothie pairs these two flavors in a delicious and healthy smoothie.

Yield: 1 serving

1 cup almond milk
1 cup frozen strawberries
1 scoop vegan chocolate protein
  powder
1 tbsp raw cacao powder

1. Add all the ingredients to a blender and blend until smooth.

2. Add some water and re-blend if necessary to achieve your desired thickness.

Chocolate Pecan Pie Protein Smoothie

If you love chocolate pecan pie, this will be a real treat for you. Low in sugar and high in protein, fiber and healthy fats, this makes a great smoothie to start the day and keep you full until lunch. Pecans and cacao nibs add a nice crunchiness to this smoothie, causing you to slow down and chew, which improves digestion of the delicious nutrients. If a crunchy smoothie isn't your thing, skip the cacao nibs and just blend until the pecans are fully blended and smooth.

Yield: 1 serving

1 cup water
1 scoop vegan chocolate
  protein powder
1/2 Medjool date, pitted
  or 1/2 frozen banana
2-4 tbsp raw pecans
1 tbsp raw cacao powder
1/2 tsp cinnamon
1/4 cup ice - optional

1. Add the water, protein powder and date or banana to a blender and blend until smooth.

2. Add a 1/4 cup of ice if using the date. No ice is necessary if using the frozen banana.

3. Add the remaining ingredients and blend until it reaches the desired consistency.

4. Blending less will yield a crunchy smoothie. Blending longer will yield a smoother one.

Note: To freeze bananas, peel first, then cut into small pieces. Spread out on a cookie sheet and place in the freezer. Once frozen, transfer the banana slices to a freezer-safe glass container. The smaller pieces of frozen banana won't stick together and will be easier for the blender to process.

NO-BAKE TREATS

Pictured: Chocolate-Covered Almond Butter Rice Cereal Bars

Chocolate Crunch Bars

These crunchy dark chocolate bars taste similar to a popular candy bar, but with almond butter flavor and much healthier ingredients. You can press these into a pan and cut into squares, or use a mini cookie scoop to make them into mini balls. Either way, if you are looking for something sweet or something with crunch, you can satisfy both with this easy-to-make treat.

Yield: 16 squares

1/4 cup organic, unrefined
  coconut oil
1/2 cup almond butter
1/4 cup 100% pure maple syrup
1/4 cup cacao powder
1/8 tsp Himalayan salt, if almond
  butter is unsalted
2 cups brown rice cereal

1. Line an 8x8 glass baking pan with parchment paper.
2. Add the coconut oil to a large glass bowl and place in an oven set to 200°F.
3. Remove the bowl as soon as the coconut oil is melted and mix in the almond butter and maple syrup.
4. If your almond butter is unsalted, add the salt and mix well.
5. Mix in the cacao powder.
6. Add in the rice cereal and mix until fully coated.
7. Press the mixture into the pan and refrigerate for 1 hour to set.
8. Remove from the pan using the parchment paper and cut into 16 squares.
9. Store in the fridge.

Chocolate-Covered Almond Butter Rice Cereal Bars

A client favorite, these rice cereal bars have a wonderful crunch
and a delicious layer of chocolate on top.

Yield: 16 squares

Bar layer:
1 cup almond butter
1/2 cup organic,
  unrefined coconut oil
1/3 cup coconut sugar
Pinch of Himalayan salt
4 cups crispy brown rice cereal

Chocolate layer:
1/2 cup chocolate chips (see note)
1/4 cup organic, unrefined
  coconut oil
1/2 cup raw cacao powder
Pinch of Himalayan salt

1. Line an 8x8 or 9x9 glass baking pan with parchment paper.
2. Add the almond butter and coconut oil to a large glass bowl and place it in an oven set to 200°F.
3. Remove the bowl from the oven when the coconut oil is melted, add the sugar and salt and mix well.
4. Add the rice cereal and mix to coat.
5. Press the mixture into the pan, spreading evenly. Place in the fridge for 2 hours, or until set.
6. Meanwhile, melt the coconut oil for the chocolate layer in a small glass bowl in the oven, then mix in the chocolate chips until thoroughly melted.
7. Mix in the cacao powder and salt and allow the mixture to cool completely. It should still be pourable, but slightly thick so that the chocolate stays on top of the bars and doesn't sink through.
8. Remove the pan from the fridge and pour the chocolate mixture over the top, spreading evenly. Return the pan to the fridge until the chocolate layer is completely hard.
9. Remove from the pan using the parchment paper and cut into 16 squares.
10. Store in the fridge.

Note: For a thicker chocolate layer, increase the chocolate chips amount by 1/4 or 1/3 cup.

Chocolate Chip Crunch Protein Bars

Do your kids love rice cereal bars, but you want them to have a snack with more protein? These bars provide a good balance of protein, carbs and healthy fats in a tasty treat that both kids and adults can appreciate.

Yield: 16 squares

1/4 cup organic, unrefined coconut oil
1/2 cup almond butter
1/4 cup honey or coconut nectar
1/4 cup vegan chocolate protein powder
2 cups brown rice cereal
1/3 cup mini chocolate chips
Pinch of Himalayan salt, if almond butter is unsalted

1. Line an 8x8 or 9x9 glass baking pan with parchment paper.
2. Add the coconut oil to a glass bowl and place in an oven set to 200°F.
3. Remove the bowl from the oven when the coconut oil is melted and mix in almond butter and honey or coconut nectar.
4. If your almond butter is unsalted, add the salt and mix in well.
5. Add the protein powder and mix well.
6. Mix in the rice cereal and chocolate chips.
7. Press into the pan and refrigerate to set.
8. Remove from the pan using the parchment paper and cut into 16 squares.
9. Store in the fridge.

Note: I don't recommend swapping maple syrup for the coconut nectar/honey because it is not as thick and the bars may have trouble sticking together.

Chocolate Mousse

This is a rich and creamy dessert that is much easier to make than traditional chocolate mousse. Adding chocolate shavings on top results in a beautiful presentation and adds a nice texture to the decadent mousse.

Yield: 2 small servings

3/4 cup canned coconut cream*
2 tbsp raw cacao powder
1 tbsp 100% pure maple syrup
Pinch of Himalayan salt
Shavings from a dark chocolate
  bar - optional

*Coconut cream is the thick cream part of canned coconut milk. For this you want regular coconut milk, not light, in a can that is free of BPA. Open the can and on top you should have coconut cream, with the coconut milk below.

1. Add all ingredients except for the chocolate shavings to a blender and blend until smooth.
2. Pour into two small dessert bowls or glasses.
3. Using a vegetable peeler across the thin edge of a chocolate bar, top each with chocolate shavings.
4. Serve immediately for a silky, soft and smooth chocolate treat.
5. If not serving immediately, store them in the fridge and they will cool and firm up.

Chocolate Coconut No-Bake Bites

These little chocolate bites are full of healthy ingredients like almond butter,
coconut, oats and cacao and are perfect for a mid-afternoon snack or a quick breakfast on the go.

Yield: 26-28 mini bites

1/2 cup almond butter
1/4 cup 100% pure maple syrup
3/4 cup unsweetened, shredded
  coconut
1/2 cup gluten-free oats
1/4 cup raw cacao powder
1 tsp vanilla
1/4 tsp Himalayan salt, if almond
  butter is unsalted

1. Add the almond butter to a glass measuring bowl and place in an oven set to 200°F.
2. Remove when warm and mix in the maple syrup and vanilla.
3. Add the remaining ingredients to a separate mixing bowl and stir to combine.
4. Add the liquid ingredients to the dry and mix until thoroughly combined. The dough will be hard to mix and will be very thick. This is important so that they stay together.
5. Using a mini cookie scoop, make individual bites. To make them into balls, roll them between your hands.
6. Store in the fridge.

Chocolate Almond Coconut Clusters

These rich and decadent treats are both creamy and crunchy.
Whether your craving is for chocolate, sugar, crunch or salt, these will satisfy.

Yield: 2 dozen mini clusters

2 tbsp raw cacao powder
3/4 cup almond butter, crunchy
3/4 cup unsweetened, shredded
  coconut
3-4 tbsp coconut sugar
Pinch of Himalayan salt, if the
  almond butter is unsalted
1/3 cup chocolate chips

1. Add the cacao powder and almond butter to a glass bowl and mix well.
2. Add the coconut, coconut sugar and salt and mix well.
3. Fold in the chocolate chips.
4. Using a mini cookie scoop, place the clusters on a parchment or silicone lined baking sheet.
5. Place in the freezer until set.
6. Store in the fridge if you like them soft or in the freezer if you like them hard.

Note: If there is a lot of oil in your almond butter, sometimes the clusters can be too moist to hold together. If that happens, you can add more coconut to the mix. Other options would be almond flour, coconut flour or freshly ground flaxseed.

Double Chocolate No-Bake Bites

These mini bites make a great between meal snack. They are full of healthy fats and complex carbs with a gentle chocolate flavor and a light hint of cinnamon. The chocolate chips add crunch and sweetness, and they store well in the fridge for an easy-to-grab, convenient snack.

Yield: 48-50 mini bites

1/4 cup coconut oil
1 cup walnuts or cashews
2 cups gluten-free oats
1/4 cup flaxseeds
1/3 cup unsweetened, shredded
  coconut
2/3 cup coconut sugar
1/4 cup raw cacao powder
1 tsp ceylon cinnamon
1/2 tsp Himalayan salt
1/2 cup almond milk
1/2 cup mini chocolate chips

1. Set the oven to 200°F.
2. Add the coconut oil to a small glass measuring bowl and place it in the oven just until melted.
3. Add the nuts to a blender and pulse a few times until they are finely ground. Pour them into a large bowl.
4. Add the oats to the blender and pulse a few times until they are ground almost into oat flour. Then add them to the bowl of ground nuts.
5. Add the flaxseeds to the blender and process until all seeds are broken. Add to the bowl.
6. Add the coconut, coconut sugar, cacao powder, cinnamon and salt to the bowl. Mix well.
7. Add the almond milk and melted coconut oil, and mix until there are no dry spots and all ingredients are well incorporated. The dough will seem too dry at first, but it eventually comes together. If necessary, add a small amount of almond milk.
8. Fold in the chocolate chips.
9. Form into bites using a mini cookie scoop.
10. Store in the fridge.

Chocolate Cream Cups

This dessert has a beautiful presentation and is a great option to serve for dessert at a dinner party. Looking much more complicated to make than they actually are, these chocolate cream cups are sure to be a hit.

Yield: 5 - 6

Chocolate cups:
1 cup chopped dark chocolate bar
  (or chocolate chips)
1 tsp organic, unrefined coconut oil

Filling:
1 cup chopped dark chocolate bar
  (or chocolate chips)
3/4 cup chilled coconut cream*

*Coconut cream is the thick cream part of canned coconut milk. For this you want regular coconut milk, not light, in a can that is free of BPA. Open the can and on top you should have coconut cream, with the coconut milk below.

1. Add the chopped dark chocolate bar and coconut oil for the chocolate cups to a glass bowl and place in an oven set to 200°F.
2. Remove when melted and stir until smooth.
3. Using a pastry brush, generously brush the melted chocolate on the inside of 5-6 silicone baking cups.
4. Once fully coated, place in the fridge for 15 minutes to set.
5. Remove the cups from the fridge and brush a second coat of chocolate on the inside of the baking cups to ensure a nice, thick chocolate cup.
6. Return the chocolate-lined cups to the fridge for an additional 15 minutes.
7. Melt the chocolate for the filling in a glass bowl in the oven set to 200°F.
8. Remove when melted and stir until smooth.
9. Gently fold in the coconut cream. If there is any leftover chocolate from making the chocolate cups, fold this in as well.
10. Gently peel back the silicone cup from the chocolate cup, being careful not to crack the delicate chocolate.
11. Using a piping bag, cookie scoop or a spoon, evenly divide the chocolate coconut cream among the chocolate cups.
12. Place in the fridge to set and store in the fridge until serving.

Creamy Chocolate Almond Butter

Nutella is a great concept, but if you are trying to eat healthy and avoid processed foods and high amounts of sugar, then try this homemade chocolate nut butter. Any kind of nut butter will work with this recipe. It is best served immediately because it does thicken up quite a bit in the fridge.

Yield: slightly over 1 cup

1/2 cup chocolate chips*
1/2 cup almond butter, or other nut butter
1/4 cup canned coconut milk**
Pinch of Himalayan salt, if nut butter is unsalted

*If you want a slightly less sweet version, you can sub a chopped dark chocolate bar for the chocolate chips. You can always add a little sweetener at the end if necessary.

**The can of coconut milk will be part liquid and part thick cream. Use half thick cream (2 tbsp) and half (2 tbsp) liquid. For more of a chocolate sauce consistency, use all liquid and no cream.

1. Add the chocolate chips and almond butter to a glass bowl and place in an oven set to 200°F.
2. Remove when the chocolate chips are melted and mix until completely smooth.
3. Add the coconut milk and mix until thoroughly incorporated, ensuring no white lumps of coconut milk are seen. To get a creamier end product, you can add more coconut milk.
4. Mix in a pinch of Himalayan salt if your nut butter is unsalted.
5. Store in the fridge.

Chocolate Coconut Crunch Bars

Creamy and crunchy at the same time, this delicious treat combines the flavors of chocolate, coconut and almond butter. For additional crunch and sweetness, press chocolate chips into the top before placing in the refrigerator.

Yield: 16 squares

1/2 cup almond butter
3 tbsp organic, unrefined
  coconut oil
1/3 cup canned coconut cream*
1/3 cup coconut sugar
1/4 cup raw cacao powder
1/8 tsp Himalayan salt, if almond
  butter is unsalted
1 cup unsweetened, shredded
  coconut
1 1/2 cups brown rice cereal

*Coconut cream is the thick cream part of canned coconut milk. For this you want regular coconut milk, not light, in a can that is free of BPA. Open the can and on top you should have coconut cream, with the coconut milk below.

1. Line an 8x8 or 9x9 glass baking pan with parchment paper.
2. Add the almond butter and coconut oil to a large glass bowl and place in an oven set to 200°F.
3. Remove the bowl from the oven when the coconut oil is melted and mix well.
4. Stir in the coconut cream, coconut sugar and cacao powder.
5. If your almond butter is unsalted, add the salt and mix in well.
6. Add the coconut and rice cereal and stir until fully coated. Press the mixture evenly into the pan.
7. Place in the fridge and allow to set for at least 30 minutes.
8. Remove from the pan using the parchment paper and cut into 16 squares.
9. Store in the fridge.

Optional: Cover with chocolate chips, pressing them in with hands or the back of a spatula.

Chocolate Pecan Date Balls

Four simple ingredients combine to create a fudgy, bite-sized snack.

Yield: varies

1 cup raw pecans
6 Medjool dates, pitted
1/4 cup raw cacao powder
1/4 tsp Himalayan salt
Mini chocolate chips - optional

1. Rinse the pecans, then soak them in filtered water for at least 1 hour and up to overnight.
2. Rinse the pecans after soaking and add them to a food processor.
3. Remove the pits from the dates and add to the food processor with the pecans, cacao powder and salt.
4. Process until it becomes a dough ball, scraping the sides as necessary.
5. Remove the blade from the processor.
6. Mix in chocolate chips, if desired.
7. Form small balls using a spoon and your hands.
8. Store in the fridge.

CANDY

Pictured: Dark Chocolate Coconut Candies (left), Dark Chocolate Walnut Candies (middle), Dark Chocolate Candies (right)

Dark Chocolate Candies

Yield: 15 candies

1/4 cup organic, unrefined
  coconut oil
1/2 cup raw cacao powder
2 tbsp 100% pure maple syrup
Pinch of Himalayan salt - optional

1. Add the coconut oil to a glass bowl and place in an oven set to 200°F.
2. Once the coconut oil is fully melted, remove from the oven and add the cacao powder. Whisk until no lumps are left.
3. Let cool for 30 minutes, then stir again. The chocolate should thicken to a nice creamy texture but still be pourable. Skipping this step will result in the maple syrup separating from the mixture.
4. Add the maple syrup and salt, if using, and stir again. Taste for sweetness and add a touch more maple syrup if necessary.
5. Pour the chocolate into silicone candy molds.
6. Gently lift and tap the candy molds on the counter until the chocolate settles evenly.
7. Place the candy molds in the refrigerator for 30 minutes, or until the chocolate is set.
8. Store in an airtight container in the fridge.

Note: If you like a softer, room-temperature chocolate, take the chocolate out of the fridge and let it sit out for a bit before enjoying. The chocolate will soften to a rich, creamy texture.

Dark Chocolate Orange Candies

Yield: 15 candies

1/4 cup organic, unrefined
  coconut oil
1/2 cup raw cacao powder
2 tbsp 100% pure maple syrup
3 drops orange extract
Pinch of Himalayan salt - optional

1. Add the coconut oil to a glass bowl and place in an oven set to 200°F.
2. Once the coconut oil is fully melted, remove from the oven and add the cacao powder. Whisk until no lumps are left.
3. Let cool for 30 minutes, then stir again. The chocolate should thicken to a nice creamy texture but still be pourable. Skipping this step will result in the maple syrup separating from the mixture.
4. Add the maple syrup, orange extract and salt, if using, and stir again. Taste for sweetness and add a touch more maple syrup if necessary.
5. Pour the chocolate into silicone candy molds.
6. Gently lift and tap the candy molds on the counter until the chocolate settles evenly.
7. Place the candy molds in the refrigerator for 30 minutes, or until the chocolate is set.
8. Store in an airtight container in the fridge.

Note: If you like a softer, room-temperature chocolate, take the chocolate out of the fridge and let it sit out for a bit before enjoying. The chocolate will soften to a rich, creamy texture.

Dark Chocolate Mint Candies

Yield: 15 candies

1/4 cup organic, unrefined
coconut oil
1/2 cup raw cacao powder
2 tbsp 100% pure maple syrup
3-5 drops organic peppermint
extract
Pinch of Himalayan salt - optional

1. Add the coconut oil to a glass bowl and place in an oven set to 200°F.
2. Once the coconut oil is fully melted, remove from the oven and add the cacao powder.
3. Whisk until no lumps are left.
4. Let cool for 30 minutes, then stir again. The chocolate should thicken to a nice creamy texture but still be pourable. Skipping this step will result in the maple syrup separating from the mixture.
5. Add the maple syrup, peppermint extract and salt, if using, and stir again. Taste for sweetness and add a touch more maple syrup if necessary.
6. Pour the chocolate into silicone candy molds.
7. Gently lift and tap the candy molds on the counter until the chocolate settles evenly.
8. Place the candy molds in the refrigerator for 30 minutes, or until the chocolate is set.
9. Store in an airtight container in the fridge.

Note: If you like a softer, room-temperature chocolate, take the chocolate out of the fridge and let it sit out for a bit before enjoying. The chocolate will soften to a rich, creamy texture.

Dark Chocolate Almond Butter Candies

Yield: 15 candies

*1/4 cup organic, unrefined
  coconut oil
1/2 cup raw cacao powder
2 tbsp 100% pure maple syrup
2 tbsp almond butter
Pinch of Himalayan sea salt, if
  almond butter is unsalted*

1. Add the coconut oil to a glass bowl and place in an oven set to 200°F.
2. Once the coconut oil is fully melted, remove from the oven and add the cacao powder.
3. Whisk until no lumps are left.
4. Add the remaining ingredients, one at a time, whisking until smooth and no lumps are left.
5. If your almond butter is unsalted, add the salt and mix well.
6. Pour the chocolate into silicone candy molds.
7. Gently lift and tap the candy molds on the counter until the chocolate settles evenly.
8. Place the candy molds in the refrigerator for 30 minutes, or until the chocolate is set.
9. Store in an airtight container in the fridge.

Note: If you like a softer, room-temperature chocolate, take the chocolate out of the fridge and let it sit out for a bit before enjoying. The chocolate will soften to a rich, creamy texture.

Dark Chocolate Crunch Candies

Yield: 15 candies

1/4 cup organic, unrefined
  coconut oil
1/2 cup raw cacao powder
2 tbsp 100% pure maple syrup
Pinch of Himalayan salt - optional
1 rounded tbsp cacao nibs,
  chopped*

*Use blended/chopped cacao nibs.
Place cacao nibs in a blender and
pulse a few times to break into
smaller pieces. See page 11 for a
special note about cacao nibs.*

1. Add the coconut oil to a glass bowl and place in an oven set to 200°F.
2. Once the coconut oil is fully melted, remove from the oven and add the cacao powder.
3. Whisk until no lumps are left.
4. Let cool for 30 minutes, then stir again. The chocolate should thicken to a nice creamy texture but still be pourable. Skipping this step will result in the maple syrup separating from the mixture.
5. Add the maple syrup and salt, if using, and stir again. Taste for sweetness and add a touch more maple syrup if necessary.
6. Stir in the cacao nibs.
7. Pour the chocolate into silicone candy molds.
8. Gently lift and tap the candy molds on the counter until the chocolate settles evenly.
9. Place the candy molds in the fridge for 30 minutes, or until the chocolate is set.
10. Store in an airtight container in the fridge.

Note: If you like a softer, room-temperature chocolate, take the chocolate out of the fridge and let it sit out for a bit before enjoying. The chocolate will soften to a rich, creamy texture.

Dark Chocolate Walnut Candies

Yield: varies

1/4 cup organic, unrefined
  coconut oil
1/2 cup raw cacao powder
2+ tbsp 100% pure maple syrup
1/8 tsp or less of pure vanilla
Pinch of Himalayan salt
1/2 cup raw walnuts, chopped

1. Add the coconut oil to a glass bowl and place in an oven set to 200°F.
2. Once the coconut oil is fully melted, remove from the oven and add the cacao powder.
3. Whisk until no lumps are left.
4. Let cool for 30 minutes, then stir again. The chocolate should thicken to a nice creamy texture but still be pourable. Skipping this step will result in the maple syrup separating from the mixture.
5. Add the maple syrup, vanilla and salt, if using, and stir again. Taste for sweetness and add a touch more maple syrup if necessary.
6. Mix in the walnuts.
7. Pour the chocolate into silicone candy molds.
8. Gently lift and tap the candy molds on the counter until the chocolate settles evenly.
9. Place the candy molds in the refrigerator for 30 minutes, or until the chocolate is set.
10. Store in an airtight container in the fridge.

Notes: If you like a softer, room-temperature chocolate, take the chocolate out of the fridge and let it sit out for a bit before enjoying. The chocolate will soften to a rich, creamy texture.

Instead of silicone molds, you can also place small spoonfuls of chocolate mixture on a silicone or parchment paper lined baking sheet. Another option is to spread into one thick rectangle (on silicone or parchment paper) and make chocolate bark (break into pieces after hardened in fridge).

Dark Chocolate Pecan Candies

Yield: varies

1/4 cup organic, unrefined
  coconut oil
1/2 cup raw cacao powder
2+ tbsp 100% pure maple syrup
Pinch of Himalayan salt, if pecans
  are unsalted
1/2 cup pecans, chopped

1. Add the coconut oil to a glass bowl and place in an oven set to 200°F.
2. Once the coconut oil is fully melted, remove from the oven and add the cacao powder.
3. Whisk until no lumps are left.
4. Let cool for 30 minutes, then stir again. The chocolate should thicken to a nice creamy texture but still be pourable. Skipping this step will result in the maple syrup separating from the mixture.
5. Add the maple syrup and salt, and stir again. Taste for sweetness and add a touch more maple syrup if necessary.
6. Mix in the pecans. They can be raw, or roasted and salted.
7. Pour the chocolate into silicone candy molds or silicone baking cups.
8. Gently lift and tap the candy molds on the counter until the chocolate settles evenly.
9. Place the candy molds in the fridge for 30 minutes, or until the chocolate is set.
10. Store in an airtight container in the refrigerator.

Note: If you like a softer, room-temperature chocolate, take the chocolate out of the fridge and let it sit out for a bit before enjoying. The chocolate will soften to a rich, creamy texture.

Dark Chocolate Coconut Candies

Yield: varies

*1/4 cup organic, unrefined
  coconut oil
1/2 cup raw cacao powder
2 tbsp 100% pure maple syrup
Pinch of Himalayan salt - optional
1/2 cup unsweetened, shredded
  coconut*

1. Add the coconut oil to a glass bowl and place in an oven set to 200°F.
2. Once the coconut oil is fully melted, remove from the oven and add the cacao powder.
3. Whisk until no lumps are left.
4. Let cool for 30 minutes, then stir again. The chocolate should thicken to a nice creamy texture but still be pourable. Skipping this step will result in the maple syrup separating from the mixture.
5. Add the maple syrup and salt, if using, and stir again. Taste for sweetness and add a touch more maple syrup if necessary.
6. Mix in the coconut.
7. Pour the chocolate into silicone candy molds.
8. Gently lift and tap the candy molds on the counter until the chocolate settles evenly.
9. Place the candy molds in the fridge for 30 minutes, or until chocolate is set.
10. Store in an airtight container in the fridge.

Note: If you like a softer, room-temperature chocolate, take the chocolate out of the fridge and let it sit out for a bit before enjoying. The chocolate will soften to a rich, creamy texture.

Dark Chocolate Macadamia Nut Clusters

Yield: 6-8 large clusters

1/4 cup organic, unrefined
  coconut oil
1/2 cup raw cacao powder
2 tbsp 100% pure maple syrup
30 roasted and salted macadamia
  nuts, lightly chopped

1. Add the coconut oil to a glass bowl and place in an oven set to 200°F.
2. Once the coconut oil is fully melted, remove from the oven and add the cacao powder.
3. Whisk until no lumps are left.
4. Let cool for 30 minutes, then stir again. The chocolate should thicken to a nice creamy texture but still be pourable. Skipping this step will result in the maple syrup separating from the mixture.
5. Add the maple syrup and stir again. Taste for sweetness and add a touch more maple syrup if necessary.
6. Mix in the macadamia nuts.
7. Evenly divide the mixture between 6 to 8 silicone muffin cups.
8. Gently lift and tap the muffin cups on the counter until the chocolate settles evenly.
9. Place in the fridge for 60 minutes, or until the chocolate is set.
10. Store in an airtight container in the fridge.

Chocolate Coconut Macadamia Nut Clusters

Yield: 6-8 large clusters

1/4 cup organic, unrefined
  coconut oil
1/2 cup raw cacao
2 tbsp 100% pure maple syrup
1/4 cup roasted and salted
  macadamia nuts, chopped
1/4 cup unsweetened, shredded
  coconut

1. Add the coconut oil to a glass bowl and place in an oven set to 200°F.
2. Once the coconut oil is fully melted, remove from the oven and add the cacao powder.
3. Whisk until no lumps are left.
4. Let cool for 30 minutes, then stir again. The chocolate should thicken to a nice creamy texture but still be pourable. Skipping this step will result in the maple syrup separating from the mixture.
5. Add the maple syrup and stir again. Taste for sweetness and add a touch more maple syrup if necessary.
6. Mix in the macadamia nuts and coconut.
7. Evenly divide the mixture between 6 to 8 silicone muffin cups.
8. Gently lift and tap the muffin cups on the counter until the chocolate settles evenly.
9. Place in the fridge for 60 minutes, or until the chocolate is set.
10. Store in an airtight container in the fridge.

Chocolate Chip Coconut Bonbons

Yield: 38-40 bonbons

Filling:
3 tbsp organic, unrefined
  coconut oil
1/2 cup almond butter
1/2 cup canned coconut cream*
1/3 cup coconut sugar
1/4 cup raw cacao powder
2 1/2 cups unsweetened, shredded
  coconut
Pinch of Himalayan salt, if almond
  butter is unsalted

Chocolate Coating:
1/4 cup organic, unrefined
  coconut oil
1 1/3 cup chocolate chips
1/2 cup raw cacao powder

**Coconut cream is the thick cream
part of canned coconut milk.
For this you want regular coconut
milk, not light, in a can that is free
of BPA. Open the can and on top
you should have coconut cream,
with the coconut milk below.*

Filling:
1. Add the coconut oil to a glass bowl and place in an oven set to 200°F.
2. Remove the bowl from the oven when the coconut oil is melted, add the almond butter and mix well.
3. Stir in the coconut cream, coconut sugar and cacao powder and mix well.
4. If your almond butter is unsalted, add the salt and mix well.
5. Add the coconut and stir until combined.
6. Using a small cookie scoop, place rounds close together on a parchment or silicone lined baking sheet.
7. Insert a toothpick in each and place in the freezer for 2 hours to harden.

Chocolate Coating:
1. After the dough balls have been in the freezer for 2 hours, place the coconut oil and chocolate chips for the chocolate coating into a glass bowl and allow to melt in an oven set to 200°F.
2. Remove the bowl and stir until smooth.
3. Add the cacao powder and mix until smooth.
4. Allow to fully cool and thicken slightly. It should be thick but still pourable.

Put it all together:
1. Remove the cookie sheet from the freezer.
2. Using the toothpick and a fork, dip the balls one at a time into the chocolate. Let the excess drip off and place the balls back on the lined cookie sheet.
3. Using a twisting motion, remove the toothpick immediately after setting each one on the tray and ensure that the hole where the toothpick was is filled in with chocolate.
4. Repeat until all are covered in chocolate.
5. If there is extra chocolate, drizzle the excess over the top of the bonbons, creating a pretty pattern.
6. Place the tray back in the fridge for 15 minutes or more to set the chocolate.
7. Store in a covered container in the fridge.

Chocolate Almond Butter Bonbons

Yield: 24-26 bonbons

Filling:
2 tbsp raw cacao powder
3 tbsp coconut sugar
3 tbsp coconut flour
1/4 tsp Himalayan salt
3/4 cup almond butter, crunchy
1/3 - 1/2 cup mini chocolate chips

Chocolate Coating:
2 tbsp organic, unrefined
* coconut oil*
2/3 cup chocolate chips
1/4 cup raw cacao powder

Filling:

1. Add the cacao powder, coconut sugar, coconut flour and salt to a glass bowl and mix well until there are no lumps.

2. Mix in the almond butter.

3. Fold in the chocolate chips.

4. Using a small cookie scoop, place balls of filling onto a parchment or silicone lined baking sheet.

5. Insert a toothpick in each and place in the freezer for 2 hours to harden.

Chocolate Coating:

1. After the dough balls have been in the freezer for 2 hours, place the coconut oil and chocolate chips for the chocolate coating into a glass bowl and allow to melt in an oven set to 200°F.

2. Remove the bowl and stir until smooth.

3. Add the cacao powder and mix until smooth.

4. Allow to fully cool and thicken slightly. It should be thick but still pourable.

Put it all together:

1. Remove the cookie sheet from the freezer.

2. Using the toothpick and a fork, dip the balls one at a time into the chocolate. Let the excess drip off and place the balls back on the lined cookie sheet.

3. Using a twisting motion, remove the toothpick immediately after setting each one on the tray and ensure that the hole where the toothpick was is filled in with chocolate.

4. Repeat until all are covered in chocolate.

5. If there is extra chocolate, drizzle the excess over the top of the bonbons, creating a pretty pattern.

6. Place the tray back in the fridge for 15 minutes or more to set the chocolate.

7. Store in a covered container in the fridge.

Dark Chocolate Almond Bark

Yield: varies

1/4 cup organic, unrefined
  coconut oil
1/2 cup raw cacao powder
2 tbsp 100% pure maple syrup
Pinch of Himalayan salt
1/4 cup sliced almonds

1. Add the coconut oil to a glass bowl and place in an oven set to 200°F.
2. Once the coconut oil is fully melted, remove from the oven and add the cacao powder. Whisk until no lumps are left.
3. Let cool for 30 minutes, then stir again. The chocolate should thicken to a nice creamy texture but still be pourable. Skipping this step will result in the maple syrup separating from the mixture.
4. Add the maple syrup and salt and stir again. Taste for sweetness and add a touch more maple syrup if necessary.
5. Mix in the almonds until all are coated.
6. Pour the mixture onto a parchment or silicone lined baking sheet. Spread using a spatula until the chocolate settles evenly to your desired thickness.
7. Place in the fridge for 30-60 minutes, or until the chocolate is set.
8. Remove and break into pieces.
9. Store in an airtight container in the fridge.

Dark Chocolate Crunch Candy Bars

Similar to a popular mainstream candy bar, these give you the taste you remember with more nutrition and less sugar.

Yield: 16 squares

1/2 cup organic, unrefined
 coconut oil
1/4 cup chocolate chips
1/2 cup plus 2 tbsp raw
 cacao powder
3-4 tbsp 100% pure maple syrup
1/8 tsp Himalayan salt
1 cup brown rice cereal

1. Line an 8x8 or 9x9 inch glass baking pan with parchment paper.
2. Add the coconut oil and chocolate chips to a glass bowl and place in an oven set to 200°F.
3. Once the coconut oil is fully melted, remove from the oven and stir until smooth.
4. Add the cacao powder and whisk until no lumps are left.
5. Let cool for 30-60 minutes, then stir again. The chocolate should thicken to a nice creamy texture but still be pourable. Skipping this step will result in the maple syrup separating from the mixture.
6. Add the maple syrup and salt, and stir again.
7. Mix in the rice cereal until fully coated.
8. Ensuring that the mixture is thick enough, pour it onto the parchment paper lined pan. You should have to spread it to the edges of the pan to get an even thickness. If it immediately spreads to the edges, it is still too thin to pour.
9. Place the pan in the fridge for a minimum of 60 minutes, or until the chocolate is completely hard.
10. Remove from the pan using the parchment paper and cut into 16 squares.
11. Store in the fridge.

Dark Chocolate Almond Butter Cups

Getting the proportions on this recipe is a little challenging,
but follow the directions closely for a healthy version of a famous classic candy.

Yield: 12 candies

Chocolate:
1/3 cup organic, unrefined
  coconut oil
2 tbsp chocolate chips
1/2 cup raw cacao powder
2 tbsp pure maple syrup

Middle Layer:
2 1/2 tbsp almond butter
1 tsp organic, unrefined
  coconut oil
1 tsp 100% pure maple syrup
Pinch of Himalayan salt, if your
  almond butter is unsalted

Chocolate:

1. Add the coconut oil and chocolate chips to a glass measuring bowl and place in an oven set to 200°F.
2. When the oil is melted, remove the bowl and mix until the chocolate chips are completely smooth.
3. Add the remaining ingredients, stirring until there are no lumps. Set aside to cool.

Middle Layer:

1. Add the almond butter and coconut oil to a glass bowl and place in an oven set to 200°F.
2. When the coconut oil is melted, remove and stir until smooth.
3. Add the maple syrup and salt, if using and mix well.

Put it all together:

1. When the chocolate has thickened, stir again to ensure the ingredients have not separated.
2. Pour the bottom layer of chocolate in 12 spots of a silicone mini muffin pan, using a little over 1/3 but not 1/2 of the chocolate. Alternatively, you could use individual silicone muffin cups. Place in the freezer for at least 10 minutes to set.
3. Place slightly less than 1 tsp of the almond butter mixture in the middle of each chocolate.
4. Place back in the freezer for at least 10 minutes to set.
5. Remove from the freezer and cover each with chocolate until flat on top.
6. Place in the freezer for 1 hour to set.
7. Remove each candy carefully to avoid cracking the chocolate.
8. Store in the fridge or freezer.

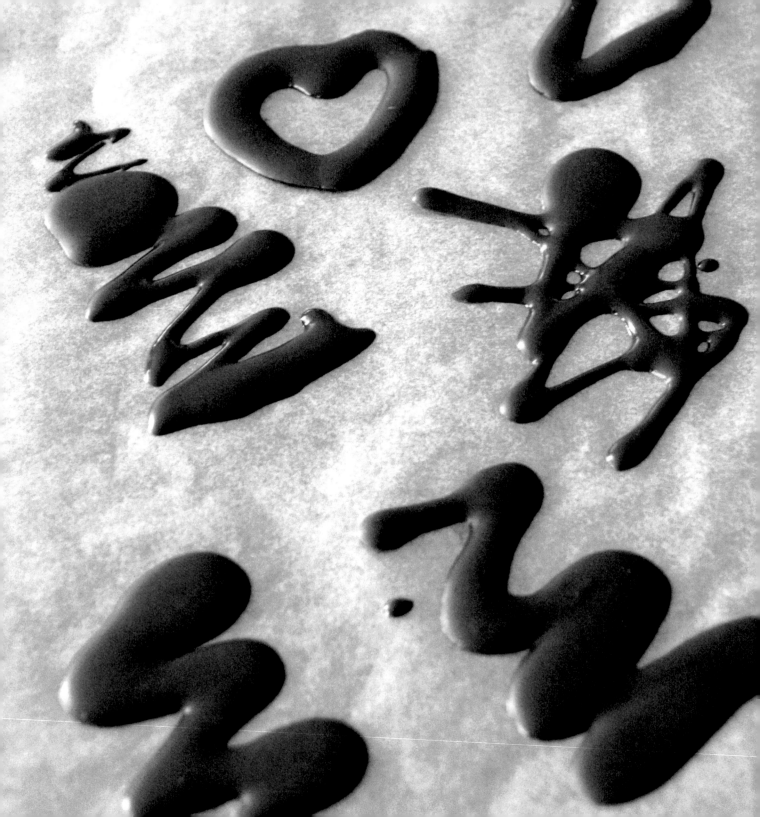

Chocolate Shapes & Letters

It is fun to add these chocolate shapes and letters to the top of a dessert for a little extra flair, especially when entertaining. These would be great to add to several of the recipes in this book, like a piece of chocolate cream pie, a frosted cupcake or even chocolate mousse.

Yield: varies

1/3 cup organic chocolate chips or
  chopped dark chocolate bar
1 tsp organic, unrefined
  coconut oil

1. Melt the ingredients in a glass bowl in an oven set to 200°F.
2. Mix the chocolate until there are no lumps. Allow the chocolate to cool slightly.
3. Ideally you want to use a squeeze bottle from a craft store to draw beautiful letters or shapes on parchment paper or a silicone lined baking sheet.
4. If you don't have one, you can use a small spoon to drizzle shapes and letters.
5. Don't worry about any stray drops. They can be removed when frozen much easier than trying to clean them up as you go.
6. Place the baking sheet in the freezer until the shapes are set.
7. Remove the shapes very carefully by peeling back the parchment paper slowly. They are very delicate and crack easily.
8. Store them in the freezer until ready to serve.

Ways to use:

1. Spell out words on a dessert plate, like "Happy Birthday," "Happy Anniversary," or a person's name.
2. Make the first letter of everyone's name to place on top of desserts when entertaining.
3. Make hearts to lay flat on top of a chocolate martini.
4. Place shapes on top of soft desserts like a frosted cupcake, ice cream or cream pie.
5. Flavor them to match your dessert by adding mint, orange or another extract.

COOKIES

Pictured: Chocolate Coconut Pecan Cookies

Chocolate Chip Macadamia Nut Cookies

This quick and simple cookie recipe is great for a lunchbox treat or an afternoon snack. They can be made in less than 20 minutes from start to finish.

Yield: 8 cookies

1/2 cup almond butter
1/4 cup coconut sugar
1 tbsp cacao powder
1 egg, preferably pastured
* and organic*
1/8 tsp Himalayan salt
3-4 tbsp chocolate chips
10 roasted and salted macadamia
* nuts, chopped*

1. Preheat the oven to 300°F.

2. Mix the first five ingredients in a small bowl.

3. Fold in the macadamia nuts and chocolate chips.

4. Using a mini cookie scoop, place the cookies about one inch apart on a parchment or silicone lined baking sheet.

5. Bake for 8 minutes.

6. Allow to fully cool before removing from the pan.

Chocolate Coconut Pecan Cookies

These cookies are good as no-bake bites and cooked, so try them both ways.
Loaded with coconut, healthy nuts and seeds, and sweetened with dates, these cookies
are healthy and delicious.

Yield: 8-10 cookies

1/2 cup raw pecans, soaked*
5 Medjool dates, pitted
1/3 cup unsweetened, shredded
  coconut
2 tbsp flax seeds, freshly ground
2 tbsp organic, unrefined
  coconut oil, soft
2 tbsp raw cacao powder
1/8 tsp Himalayan salt
3-4 tbsp chocolate chips

*Pecans can be soaked for as little
as 1 hour to as much as overnight.
Place them in a bowl and cover
with water. Drain and rinse before
using.

1. Preheat the oven to 300°F.
2. Remove the pits from the dates and add to a food processor with the pecans. Process for 30-60 seconds.
3. Add the remaining ingredients, except for the chocolate chips. The coconut oil should be soft, so if it is hard, place it in the preheating oven for a few minutes until soft, but not melted.
4. Process the mixture until combined, scraping down the sides as necessary. The end product should be a moist, thick, slightly chunky dough.
5. Remove the blade and mix in the chocolate chips.
6. Using a cookie scoop, place the cookies on a parchment or silicone lined baking sheet.
7. Bake for 8 minutes.
8. Allow to fully cool before removing from the pan.

Chocolate Almond Butter Thumbprint Cookies

These cookies are so simple to make. There are just four ingredients to the cookie and two for the chocolate center.

Yield: 7-8 cookies

3 tbsp chocolate chips
1/2 tsp organic, unrefined
  coconut oil
1/2 cup almond butter
3 tbsp coconut sugar
1 egg, preferably pastured
  and organic
1/8 tsp Himalayan salt

1. Preheat the oven to 325°F.
2. Put the chocolate chips and coconut oil in a small glass bowl and place in the preheating oven until the coconut oil is melted. Stir until smooth and set the bowl aside.
3. Add the almond butter and coconut sugar to a small glass bowl and mix well.
4. Add the egg and salt and mix well. Double the amount of salt if the almond butter is unsalted. The dough will be very thick.
5. Using a large cookie scoop, place cookies on a parchment or silicone lined baking sheet, flattening each with the back of a silicone spatula.
6. Make a well in the center of each cookie by pressing in with your thumb.
7. Bake for 8 minutes.
8. Remove the cookies from the oven when done and allow to cool.
9. Fill the well of each cookie with chocolate and allow them to cool until the chocolate is set. Placing the cookies in the fridge will speed the process of setting the chocolate.

Creamy Chocolate Macaroons

Combining three different kinds of coconut (shredded, nectar and cream), these macaroons have a strong coconut flavor. Creamier than a traditional macaroon, they also have a strong and rich chocolate flavor.

Yield: 28-30 cookies

2 tbsp unrefined, organic
  coconut oil
1/3 cup chocolate chips
1/3 cup canned coconut cream*
1/4 cup coconut nectar
1/4 cup raw cacao powder
2 cups shredded, unsweetened
  coconut
1/4 tsp Himalayan salt

Coconut cream is the thick cream part of canned coconut milk. For this you want regular coconut milk, not light, in a can that is free of BPA. Open the can and on top you should have coconut cream, with the coconut milk below.

1. Preheat the oven to 300°F.
2. Add the chocolate chips and coconut oil to a large glass bowl and place it in the preheating oven just until melted.
3. Remove from the oven and stir until smooth.
4. Add in the coconut cream and coconut nectar and mix well.
5. Stir in the cacao, coconut and salt until well incorporated.
6. Using a small cookie scoop, place cookies close together on parchment or silicone lined baking sheet. They will not spread.
7. Bake for 12-14 minutes, or until slightly dry to the touch. They will still be soft, but do not over-cook them. They will harden up as they cool. The longer you cook them, the crunchier they will be.
8. Allow to fully cool before removing from the pan.

Chocolate Cashew Coconut Cookies

Combining the two delicious flavors of chocolate and coconut,
these macaroons are rich and creamy due to the cashews.

Yield: 18-20 cookies

1 cup cashews
1/2 cup unsweetened, shredded
  coconut
3 tbsp raw cacao powder
3 tbsp 100% pure maple syrup
1/4 tsp Himalayan salt

1. Add the cashews to a bowl and cover with water. Soak for at least 2 hours but not more than 4 hours.
2. Strain and rinse the cashews and pour into a food processor.
3. Preheat the oven to 300°F.
4. Blend the cashews in the food processor for 1 minute, until smooth.
5. Add the coconut, cacao powder, maple syrup and salt and process until blended, scraping down the sides as necessary.
6. Taste for sweetness. Add a little more maple syrup if you like a sweeter cookie.
7. Use a mini cookie scoop to place macaroons close together on a parchment or silicone lined baking sheet. They will not spread.
8. Bake for 10 minutes.
9. Allow to fully cool before removing from the pan.

BROWNIES & BARS

Pictured: Chocolate Pecan Date Squares

Chocolate Pecan Date Brownies

These delicious and moist cake-like brownies use no flour, no refined sugar and
no oil, except to coat the pan.

Yield: 16 brownies

2 1/2 cups raw pecans, soaked*
14 Medjool dates, pitted
1/2 cup canned coconut cream**
1/3 cup raw cacao powder
1/2 tsp Himalayan salt
1/2 tsp baking soda
2 eggs, preferably pastured
  and organic
1/2 cup chocolate chips
Coconut oil to coat the pan

*Pecans can be soaked for as little
as 1 hour to as much as overnight.
Place them in a bowl and cover
with water. Drain and rinse before
using.

*Coconut cream is the thick cream
part of canned coconut milk. For
this you want regular coconut milk,
not light, in a can that is free of
BPA. Open the can and on top you
should have coconut cream, with
the coconut milk below.

1. Preheat oven to 300°F.
2. Add the pecans and dates to a food processor and process until thoroughly combined and smooth, scraping down the sides as necessary. This will take several minutes.
3. Add the coconut cream and process until smooth.
4. Add the cacao powder, salt, baking soda and eggs and process until incorporated.
5. Remove the blade and mix in the chocolate chips.
6. Generously coat the bottom and sides of a 9x9 glass baking pan with coconut oil.
7. Pour the brownie dough into the pan, spreading it out evenly with a spatula.
8. Bake for 30-35 minutes, or until a toothpick inserted in the center comes out clean.
9. Allow to fully cool before slicing.

Chocolate Pecan Date Squares

These bars are so rich and moist, they almost taste raw. And they probably could be since they are made without eggs. Using pecans and cacao powder as the base, they are grain-free. Sweetened with dates, they hold together well and taste so good you won't believe how healthy they are.

Yield: 16 squares

Chocolate Layer:
1/3 cup plus 1 tbsp chocolate
  chips
1 tbsp organic, unrefined
  coconut oil
1/4 cup raw cacao powder

Base:
2 cups raw pecans, soaked*
1 cup Medjool dates, pitted
1/3 cup raw cacao powder
1/4 tsp Himalayan salt

Pecans can be soaked for as little as 1 hour to as much as overnight. Place them in a bowl and cover with water. Drain and rinse before using.

1. Preheat the oven to 300°F.
2. Add the coconut oil and chocolate chips to a glass bowl and place in the preheating oven.
3. Remove the bowl when the coconut oil is melted and stir until the chocolate chips are smooth. Mix in the cacao powder. Set aside to cool while making the bottom layer.
4. Add the pecans, dates, cacao powder and salt to a food processor and process until thoroughly combined and smooth, scraping down the sides as necessary.
5. Line the bottom of an 8x8 or 9x9 glass baking pan with parchment paper.
6. Press the dough into the pan, using a silicone spatula to spread evenly and make smooth. The dough is very thick.
7. Bake for 10 minutes.
8. Remove from the oven and allow to cool.
9. Once cool, spread the chocolate evenly over the top.
10. Place in the freezer for 30 minutes or until the chocolate has hardened.
11. Remove from the pan using the parchment paper and cut into 16 squares.
12. Store in the fridge (this keeps the chocolate from getting soft).

Chocolate Walnut Zucchini Brownies

Who knew brownies could be so healthy and still so delicious?
These grain-free and dairy-free brownies incorporate zucchini and walnuts, and
use coconut flour, which is high in fiber.

Yield: 16 brownies

1 small organic zucchini
1 cup raw walnuts, soaked*
1/2 cup organic, unrefined
  coconut oil
1/2 cup coconut sugar
3/4 cup raw cacao powder
1/2 cup coconut flour
2 eggs, preferably pastured
  and organic
1/2 tsp Himalayan salt
1/2 tsp baking soda
1/2 cup chocolate chips

*Walnuts can be soaked for as little
as 1 hour to as much as overnight.
Place them in a bowl and cover
with water. Drain and rinse before
using.

1. Preheat the oven to 350°F.
2. Cut the zucchini into a few chunks and add them to the food processor. Process until the zucchini is shredded into small pieces and there are no large chunks left.
3. Add the walnuts and process until smooth, scraping down the sides as necessary.
4. Add the remaining ingredients, except for the chocolate chips, and process until smooth.
5. Remove the blade and fold in the chocolate chips.
6. Generously coat the bottom and sides of a 9x9 glass baking pan with coconut oil.
7. Pour the dough into the pan, spreading it evenly.
8. Bake for 25-30 minutes, or until a toothpick inserted into the center comes out clean.
9. Allow to fully cool before slicing.

PIES & CAKES

Chocolate Frosting

Frosting is usually made almost entirely out of processed sugar and other unhealthy ingredients. This frosting starts with chocolate and cacao powder, is softened with coconut cream, and is sweetened with dates. Although it is not low in sugar, it is a much healthier frosting option.

Yield: 2 cups

8 Medjool dates, pitted
1/2 cup chocolate chips
3/4 cup canned coconut cream*
1/4 cup raw cacao powder
1/8 tsp Himalayan salt

Coconut cream is the thick cream part of canned coconut milk. For this you want regular coconut milk, not light, in a can that is free of BPA. Open the can and on top you should have coconut cream, with the coconut milk below.

1. Remove the pits from the dates and place in a small bowl. Press the dates down and add just enough filtered water to cover them. Allow them to soak for 1-2 hours.
2. Add the chocolate chips to a medium-sized glass bowl and place in an oven set to 200°F until melted.
3. Remove the dates from the water and place in a food processor and blend, scraping down the sides as necessary. Save the date-sweetened water for a smoothie or other purpose.
4. Add the coconut cream to the melted chocolate chips and mix well. Add the mixture to the food processor and blend for 1 minute to smooth out the dates completely.
5. Place the remaining ingredients in the food processor and process until the mixture is completely smooth, scraping down the sides a few times.
6. Remove the blade and place the processor bowl in the fridge for 1 hour. The frosting will harden.
7. Whether the frosting is on a dessert or not, store it in the fridge or it will become extremely soft.

Chocolate Pie Crust

Made with pecans and cacao powder and sweetened with dates, this pie crust recipe offers a lot more nutrition than traditional crusts. The two pie recipes that follow both use this crust as a base.

Yield: 1 pie crust

1 1/4 cup raw pecans, soaked*
7 Medjool dates, pitted
  (about 3/4 cup)
2 tbsp raw cacao powder
1/4 tsp Himalayan salt
Coconut oil to coat pie pan

*Pecans can be soaked for as little as 1 hour to as much as overnight. Place them in a bowl and cover with water. Drain and rinse before using.

1. Preheat the oven to 300°F.
2. Add all the ingredients to a food processor and process until thoroughly combined, scraping down the sides as necessary.
3. Generously coat a glass pie pan with coconut oil.
4. Press the crust into the pan with your fingers, then use a silicone spatula to smooth and even out the crust, pressing all the way to the edge and up the sides of the pan.
5. Bake for 15 minutes.
6. Remove from the oven and allow to cool before adding pie filling.

Chocolate Cream Pie

This silky rich pie is a perfect dessert to serve when entertaining.
The crunchy crust contrasts with the smooth filling to create a decadent treat.

Yield: 1 pie

Crust:
1 1/4 cup raw pecans, soaked*
7 Medjool dates, pitted
 (about 3/4 cup)
2 tbsp raw cacao powder
1/4 tsp Himalayan salt
Coconut oil to coat pie pan

Filling:
1 cup 70% or higher dark chocolate
 chips, chunks or chopped bar
3/4 cup canned coconut cream**
1 tbsp almond milk - optional

**Pecans can be soaked for as little
as 1 hour to as much as overnight.
Place them in a bowl and cover with
water. Drain and rinse before using.*

***Coconut cream is the thick cream
part of canned coconut milk. For
this you want regular coconut milk,
not light, in a can that is free of
BPA. Open the can and on top you
should have coconut cream, with
the coconut milk below. Scoop out
3/4 cup of coconut cream, using a
second can if necessary. You can
save the liquid to be used in a soup
or smoothie.*

1. Preheat the oven to 300°F.
2. Add all the crust ingredients to a food processor and process until thoroughly combined, scraping down the sides as necessary.
3. Generously coat the bottom and sides of a glass pie pan with coconut oil.
4. Spread the crust into the pie pan with your fingers, then use a silicone spatula to smooth and even out the crust, pressing all the way to the edge and up the sides of the pan.
5. Bake for 15 minutes.
6. Remove from the oven and allow to cool before adding pie filling.
7. While the crust is still cooking, add the chocolate for the filling into a glass bowl and place in the oven until melted.
8. Stir the melted chocolate until smooth.
9. Fold in the coconut cream until fully incorporated. Only add the almond milk if the mixture is too thick.
10. Pour the chocolate coconut cream onto the cooled pie crust.
11. Place in the fridge until the filling is set and store in the fridge until serving.

Chocolate Pecan Pie

Yield: 1 pie

Chocolate Crust:
1 1/4 cup raw pecans, soaked*
7 Medjool dates, pitted
(about 3/4 cup)
2 tbsp raw cacao powder
1/4 tsp Himalayan salt
Coconut oil to coat pie pan

Filling:
1 cup chocolate chunks or
chopped dark chocolate bar
2 tbsp organic, unrefined
coconut oil
3 eggs, preferably pastured
and organic
1 tsp vanilla
1/4 tsp Himalayan salt
1 cup pecans, soaked*

*Pecans can be soaked for as little
as 1 hour to as much as overnight.
Place them in a bowl and cover
with water. Drain and rinse before
using.

1. Preheat the oven to 300°F.
2. Add all the crust ingredients to a food processor and process until thoroughly combined, scraping down the sides as necessary.
3. Generously coat the bottom and sides of a glass pie pan with coconut oil.
4. Press the crust into the pie pan with your fingers, then use a silicone spatula to smooth and even out the crust, pressing all the way to the edge and up the sides of the pan.
5. Bake for 15 minutes.
6. Remove from the oven and allow to cool before adding pie filling.
7. While the crust is still cooking, add half the chocolate and the coconut oil to a glass bowl and place in the oven until the coconut oil is melted.
8. Remove the bowl from the oven and pour the contents into the food processor.
9. Add the eggs, vanilla and salt. Process until the eggs are blended.
10. Add the pecans and remaining chocolate chunks and process until pecans are chopped into small pieces.
11. Pour the filling into the pie crust and bake for 15 minutes or until a toothpick inserted in the center comes out clean.

Double Chocolate Cupcakes

Instead of a traditional grain flour, these cupcakes are made with ground walnuts and cacao powder, making this a healthy and delicious cupcake.

Yield: 12 mini cupcakes

Dry Ingredients:
1 cup raw walnuts
1/3 cup raw cacao powder
1/2 tsp baking soda
1/8 tsp sea salt
1/3 cup chocolate chunks

Wet Ingredients:
1 egg, preferably pastured
  and organic
1/4 cup 100% pure maple syrup
1 tsp vanilla

1. Soak walnuts in water for 4-6 hours, then drain and rinse.
2. Preheat the oven to 350°F.
3. Line a mini muffin pan with 12 parchment paper baking cups.
4. Put the walnuts in a food processor and process until they are very finely ground, stopping before they turn into nut butter.
5. Scrape down the sides, add the next three dry ingredients and pulse again to combine.
6. Add the wet ingredients and process again until smooth, scraping the sides as necessary. You may still have tiny chunks of walnuts visible, and this is fine.
7. Remove the blade and mix in the chocolate chunks.
8. Using a cookie scoop, evenly divide the batter among 12 muffin cups.
9. Bake for 13-15 minutes or until a toothpick inserted in the center comes out clean.
10. Remove from oven and allow to cool before serving.

Mini Chocolate Protein Cakes

These mini cakes are full of protein from eggs and protein powder.
Sweetened with applesauce and maple syrup, they have a subtle sweetness.
They are a great option for an afternoon snack, a lunchbox treat, or even for breakfast.

Yield: 4 mini cakes

1 tsp organic unrefined coconut oil
2 eggs, pastured and organic
1/4 cup vegan chocolate protein
  powder
3 tbsp cacao powder
3 tbsp unsweetened organic
  apple sauce
2-3 tbsp 100% pure maple syrup
1/2 tsp baking soda

1. Preheat the oven to 350°F.

2. Using a 1/4 tsp measuring spoon, divide the coconut oil among four oven-safe ramekins and place in the preheating oven.

3. Whisk eggs in a glass bowl.

4. Add the remaining ingredients and mix until fully incorporated.

5. Remove the ramekins from the oven when the coconut oil is fully melted. Turn each ramekin to ensure all sides are coated with the coconut oil. Add any excess oil to the bowl and mix in.

6. Divide the batter among the four ramekins.

7. Bake for 12-14 minutes, or until a toothpick inserted in the center comes out clean.

8. Turn ramekins over and the cakes should drop out.

9. Turn over and allow to cool.

Note: These can be served alone, with frosting, or with a chocolate sauce as shown in the picture.

Chocolate Coconut Flour Cupcakes

These cupcakes are full of fiber and nutrients from the coconut flour and cacao powder. They also have plenty of healthy fats and a little protein from the eggs. They are a great lunchbox snack without the frosting, or as a more decadent dessert with chocolate frosting on top.

Yield: 8 cupcakes

3 eggs, preferably pastured and organic
1/3 cup organic, unrefined coconut oil
1/4 cup chocolate chips
1/4 cup 100% pure maple syrup
1/4 cup raw cacao powder
1/4 cup coconut flour
1/2 tsp baking soda
1/2 tsp Himalayan salt

1. Preheat the oven to 350°F.
2. Whisk room-temperature eggs in a large glass bowl and set aside.
3. Add coconut oil and chocolate chips to a glass bowl and place in the preheating oven.
4. Once the coconut oil is melted, remove the bowl and mix well. Add the cacao powder and maple syrup, and mix until incorporated.
5. Add the mixture to the eggs and use a hand mixer to combine.
6. Add the remaining ingredients to the bowl and mix well.
7. Divide the batter among eight silicone or parchment lined muffin cups.
8. Bake for 15-20 minutes, or until a toothpick inserted in the center comes out clean.
9. Cool and then frost.

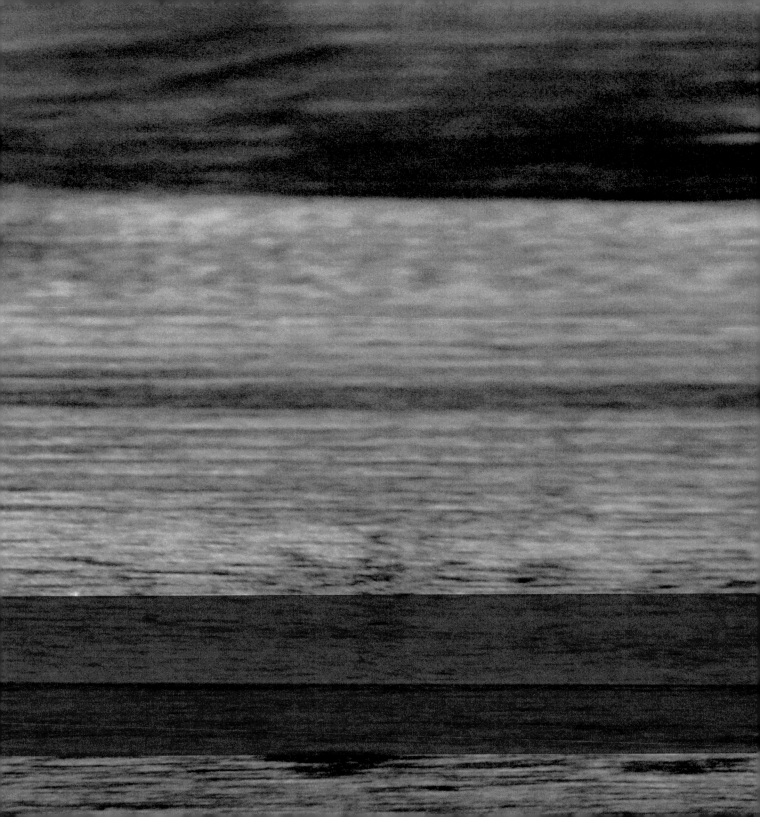

FROZEN TREATS

Pictured: Chocolate Brownie Ice "Cream"

Chocolate Ice "Cream"

This non-dairy ice cream is rich and creamy, and is quick and easy to make.
It is a great option for a summer afternoon snack.

Yield: 4 servings

1 13.5 oz can of coconut milk*
1 cup almond milk
1/4 cup raw cacao powder
1/4 cup 100% pure maple syrup
1/4 cup chocolate chips - optional

*Use regular coconut milk, not light.

1. Add all ingredients except for the chocolate chips to a blender.
2. Blend until smooth.
3. Transfer ingredients to an ice cream maker and follow the machine directions until ice cream forms.
4. Add chocolate chips, if using, in the last few minutes.
5. This ice cream is best served immediately, but if you have any leftover, store it in the freezer in a freezer-safe container.

Note: The consistency of this ice cream is like soft serve. If you like a harder ice cream, place the finished product into the freezer for at least 30 minutes, until it reaches your desired consistency.

Chocolate Mint Chip Ice "Cream"

This recipe takes the chocolate ice "cream" to another level with the flavor of peppermint and the crunch of chocolate chips.

Yield: 4 servings

1 13.5 oz can of coconut milk*
1 cup almond milk
1/4 cup raw cacao powder
1/4 cup 100% pure maple syrup
3/4 tsp peppermint extract
Pinch of Himalayan salt
1/3 cup chocolate chips

Use regular coconut milk, not light.

1. Add all the ingredients except for the chocolate chips to a blender.
2. Blend until smooth. Taste and add more peppermint extract if you'd like more mint flavor.
3. Transfer the ingredients to an ice cream maker and follow the machine directions until ice cream forms.
4. Add chocolate chips in the last few minutes.
5. This ice cream is best served immediately, but if you have any leftover, store it in the freezer in a freezer-safe container.

Note: The consistency of this ice cream is like soft serve. If you like a harder ice cream, place the finished product into the freezer for at least 30 minutes, until it reaches your desired consistency.

Chocolate Brownie Ice "Cream"

If you have some leftover brownies, this is a great way to make a fancy chocolate brownie ice cream. It works very well with the chocolate pecan brownies from this cookbook.

Yield: 5-6 servings

1 13.5 oz can of coconut milk*
1 cup almond milk
1/4 cup raw cacao powder
1/4 cup 100% pure maple syrup
Up to 1 cup of crushed brownie
  pieces

*Use regular coconut milk, not light.

1. Add the first four ingredients to a blender.
2. Blend until smooth.
3. Transfer the ingredients to an ice cream maker and follow the machine directions until ice cream forms.
4. When the ice cream looks done, add the crumbled brownies to the top and allow them to be mixed in.
5. This ice cream is best served immediately, but if you have any leftover, store it in the freezer in a freezer-safe container.

Note: The consistency of this ice cream is like soft serve. If you like a harder ice cream, place the finished product into the freezer for at least 30 minutes, until it reaches your desired consistency.

Chocolate Fudge Popsicles

These rich and creamy chocolate fudge popsicles are quick and easy to
make in any popsicle molds you have.

Yield: 3 popsicles

1 cup canned coconut milk
1/4 cup raw cacao powder
2 tbsp raw local honey
Pinch Himalayan salt

1. When measuring the cup of coconut milk, try to get about half
   of the thick cream on top and half of the thinner liquid from the
   bottom of the can.
2. Add the coconut milk and the remaining ingredients to a
   blender and blend until smooth.
3. Pour into popsicle molds and place in freezer until frozen.

Chocolate-Covered Banana Pops

This is a fun treat, combining the richness of dark chocolate and the sweetness of banana. There is a lot of flexibility with the banana-to-chocolate ratio. To have more chocolate and less banana, slice the banana thin and allow the chocolate to thicken before dipping, which will create a thicker chocolate layer. To have more banana and less chocolate, slice the banana thicker. Depending on the method you choose, you may have leftover banana slices or leftover chocolate.

Yield: varies

2 bananas
1/4 cup organic, unrefined
  coconut oil
1/2 cup raw cacao powder
2 tbsp 100% pure maple syrup
Pinch of Himalayan salt - optional

1. Peel and slice the bananas about 1/2 inch thick.
2. Stick a lollipop or popsicle stick into the side of each banana slice and place on a parchment or silicone lined baking sheet.
3. Freeze for at least 1 hour.
4. While the bananas are freezing, add the coconut oil to a glass bowl and place in an oven set to 200°F.
5. Once the coconut oil is fully melted, remove from the oven and add the cacao powder. Whisk until no lumps are left.
6. Let cool for 30 minutes, then stir again. The chocolate should thicken to a nice creamy texture but still be pourable. Skipping this step will result in the maple syrup separating from the mixture.
7. Add the maple syrup and salt, if using, and stir again. Taste for sweetness and add a touch more maple syrup if necessary.
8. Allow the chocolate to thicken while the bananas are freezing. The thicker the chocolate gets, the thicker the chocolate coating will be on each banana slice. The thicker the chocolate coating on each, the fewer banana pops will be made.
9. Remove the bananas from the freezer and dip each one into the chocolate. Allow excess chocolate to drip off (if the chocolate is thick, none will drip) and place each back on the lined baking sheet. The chocolate should start to harden immediately.
10. Place the cookie sheet back in the freezer until the chocolate is completely set.
11. Store in the freezer.
12. Take out of the freezer a couple of minutes before serving to allow banana to soften slightly.

HOT CHOCOLATE

Pictured: Almond Butter Hot Chocolate

Hot Chocolate Protein Smoothie

If you want to have a smoothie on a cold winter morning, this is the perfect choice. Combining protein with warm chocolate non-dairy milks and creams, this rich and creamy hot chocolate protein smoothie will warm you up and fill you up.

Yield: 1-2 servings

1 1/4 cup almond milk
1/4 cup canned coconut cream*
1 scoop vegan chocolate
  protein powder
2 tbsp chocolate chips

*Coconut cream is the thick cream part of canned coconut milk. For this you want regular coconut milk, not light, in a can that is free of BPA. Open the can and on top you should have coconut cream, with

1. Add all the ingredients to a blender and blend.

2. Transfer to a stainless steel pot and heat until warm.

Note: If you have a Vitamix, blend on the warm soup setting until warm.

Hot Chocolate

For those that love hot chocolate but don't eat dairy, this hot chocolate recipe combines non-dairy milk and cream with chocolate to create a rich and creamy treat.

Yield: 1 serving

2/3 cup almond milk
1/3 cup canned coconut cream*
2 tbsp raw cacao powder
1 tbsp 100% pure maple syrup

*Coconut cream is the thick cream part of canned coconut milk. For this you want regular coconut milk, not light, in a can that is free of BPA. Open the can and on top you should have coconut cream, with the coconut milk below.

1. Add all the ingredients to a blender and blend until smooth.

2. Transfer to a stainless steel pot and heat until warm.

Note: If you have a Vitamix, blend on the warm soup setting until warm.

Cinnamon Vanilla Hot Chocolate

This hot chocolate uses warm spices that go well with chocolate to create a unique hot chocolate treat.

Yield: 1 serving

2/3 cup almond milk
1/3 cup canned coconut cream*
2 tbsp raw cacao powder
1 tbsp 100% pure maple syrup
1/4 tsp cinnamon
1/4 tsp vanilla

*Coconut cream is the thick cream part of canned coconut milk. For this you want regular coconut milk, not light, in a can that is free of BPA. Open the can and on top you should have coconut cream, with the coconut milk below.

1. Add all the ingredients to a blender and blend.

2. Transfer to a stainless steel pot and heat until warm.

Note: If you have a Vitamix, blend on the warm soup setting until warm.

Mint Hot chocolate

If you love the combination of mint and dark chocolate,
then this hot chocolate recipe is for you.

Yield: 1 serving

2/3 cup almond milk
1/3 cup canned coconut cream*
2 tbsp raw cacao powder
1 tbsp 100% pure maple syrup
1/8 tsp peppermint extract

**Coconut cream is the thick cream
part of canned coconut milk. For
this you want regular coconut milk,
not light, in a can that is free of BPA.
Open the can and on top you should
have coconut cream, with the coconut
milk below.*

1. Add all the ingredients to a blender and blend.

2. Transfer to a stainless steel pot and heat until warm.

Note: If you have a Vitamix, blend on the warm soup setting until warm.

Almond Butter Hot Chocolate

If you love the flavors of almond butter and chocolate together,
then this hot chocolate is for you.

Yield: 1 serving

2/3 cup almond milk
1/3 cup canned coconut cream*
2 tbsp raw cacao powder
1 tbsp almond butter
1 tbsp 100% pure maple syrup
Pinch of Himalayan salt,
  if almond butter is unsalted

**Coconut cream is the thick cream
part of canned coconut milk. For
this you want regular coconut milk,
not light, in a can that is free of BPA.
Open the can and on top you should
have coconut cream, with the coconut
milk below.*

1. Add all the ingredients to a blender and blend.

2. Transfer to a stainless steel pot and heat until warm.

Note: If you have a Vitamix, blend on the warm soup setting until warm.

Index

*Denotes beginning of chapter